AUGUST REVERIE
Adult Coloring Book

Copyright © 2017 Vivid Publishers / Chinthaka Herath
Illustrated by Chinthaka Herath
Design & layout by Intense Media

All rights reserved. No part of this publication may be reproduced, distributed or transmitted in any form or by any means including photocopying, recording or other electronic or mechanical methods, without the prior written permission of the Publisher/ Chinthaka Herath.

ISBN-13: 978-1979783439
ISBN-10: 1979783438

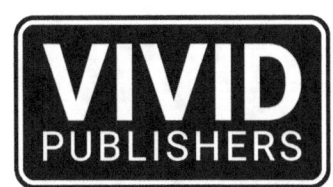

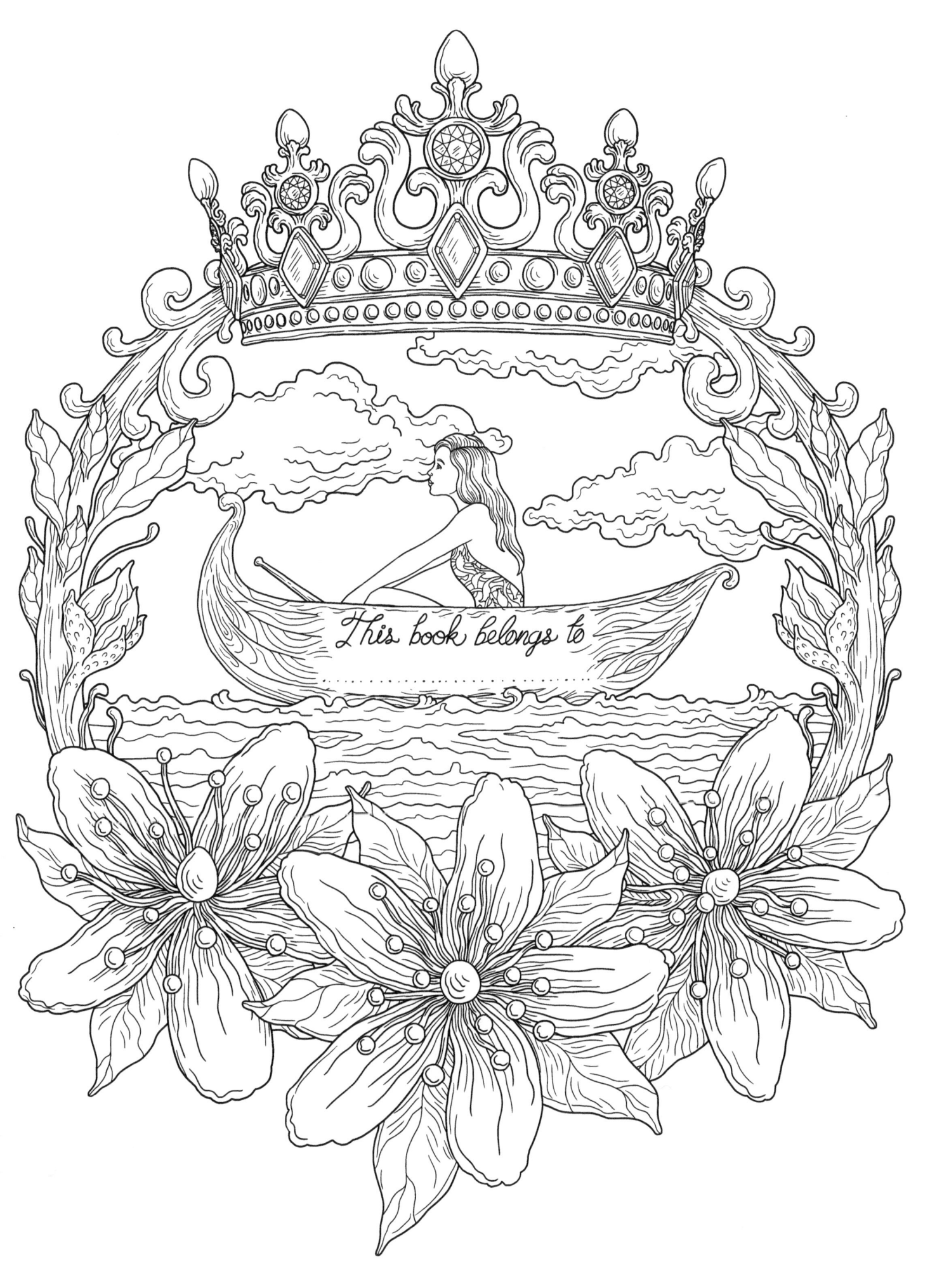

INTRODUCTION

Thank you for purchasing our adult coloring book 'August Reverie'. You will find here twenty four intricate line art drawings for your coloring pleasure.

All art is hand drawn & line art shading is included as a guide to add shadowing & lighting.

You can use any coloring medium from pencils to markers as long as they have a fine tip.

A note on the use of markers: *Even though the illustrations are printed one per page, to give additional protection please place a thick paper or cardboard beneath the page you are coloring so that the ink will not bleed through to the next page.*

Subscribe at our website to get a FREE PDF Sampler featuring pages from our other adult coloring book releases! *Plus, news on discounts, free pages, contests and more!*

 *www.vividpublishers.com*

We would love to see your completed art. You can reach us at:

 *fb.com/VividPublishers*

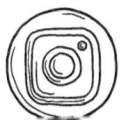 *@VividPublishers*

Also, we welcome you to join our Facebook group to share your art, see other colorists' art, enter exciting contests plus more!

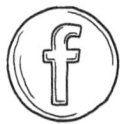 *fb.com/groups/VividPublishers*

Thank you for your continued support and interest in our adult coloring books. We hope you enjoy coloring the pages as much as we did creating them. Happy Coloring!

CONTENTS

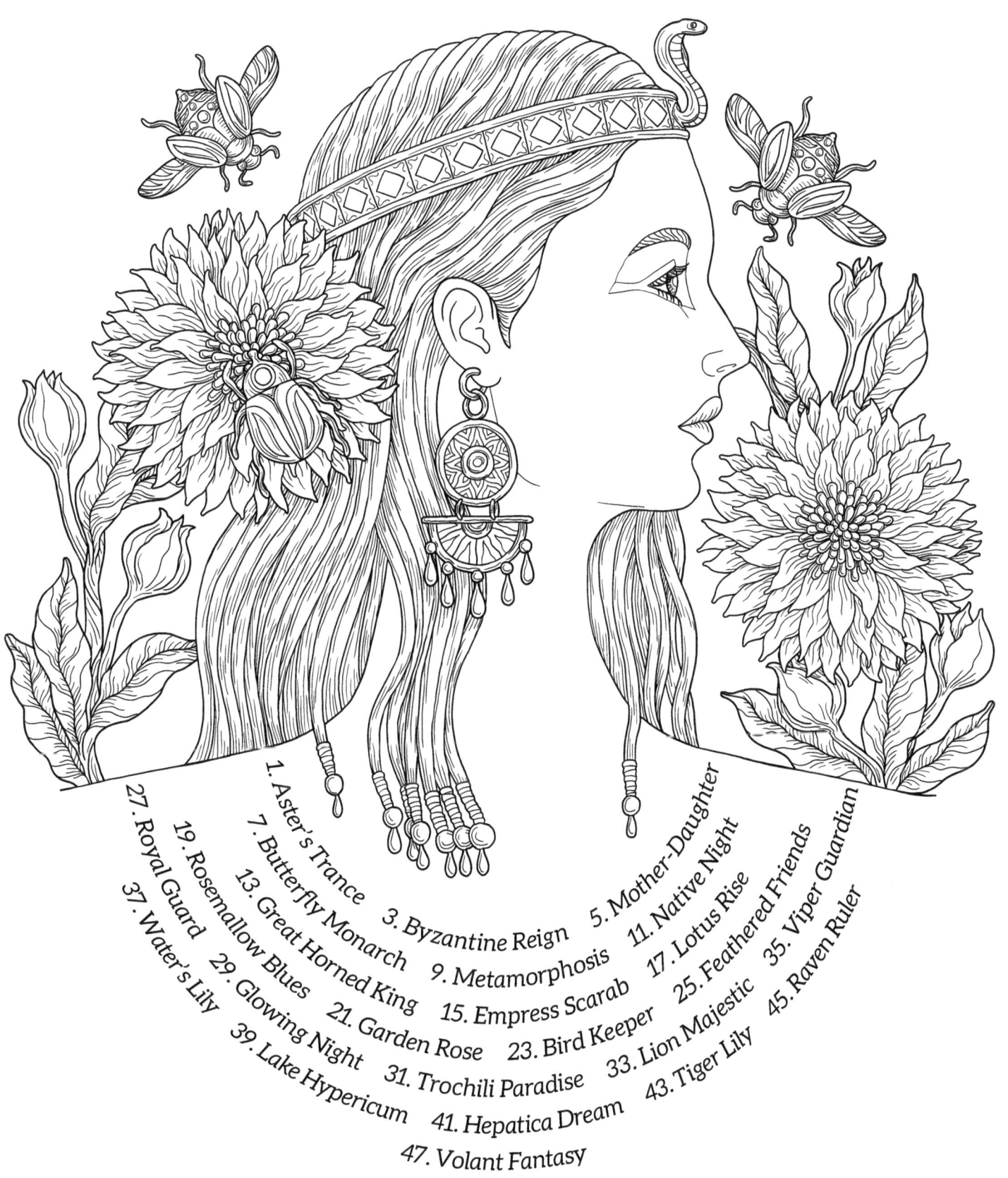

1. Aster's Trance 3. Byzantine Reign 5. Mother-Daughter
7. Butterfly Monarch 9. Metamorphosis 11. Native Night
13. Great Horned King 15. Empress Scarab 17. Lotus Rise
19. Rosemallow Blues 21. Garden Rose 23. Bird Keeper 25. Feathered Friends 35. Viper Guardian
27. Royal Guard 29. Glowing Night 31. Trochili Paradise 33. Lion Majestic 45. Raven Ruler
37. Water's Lily 39. Lake Hypericum 41. Hepatica Dream 43. Tiger Lily
47. Volant Fantasy

Aster's Trance

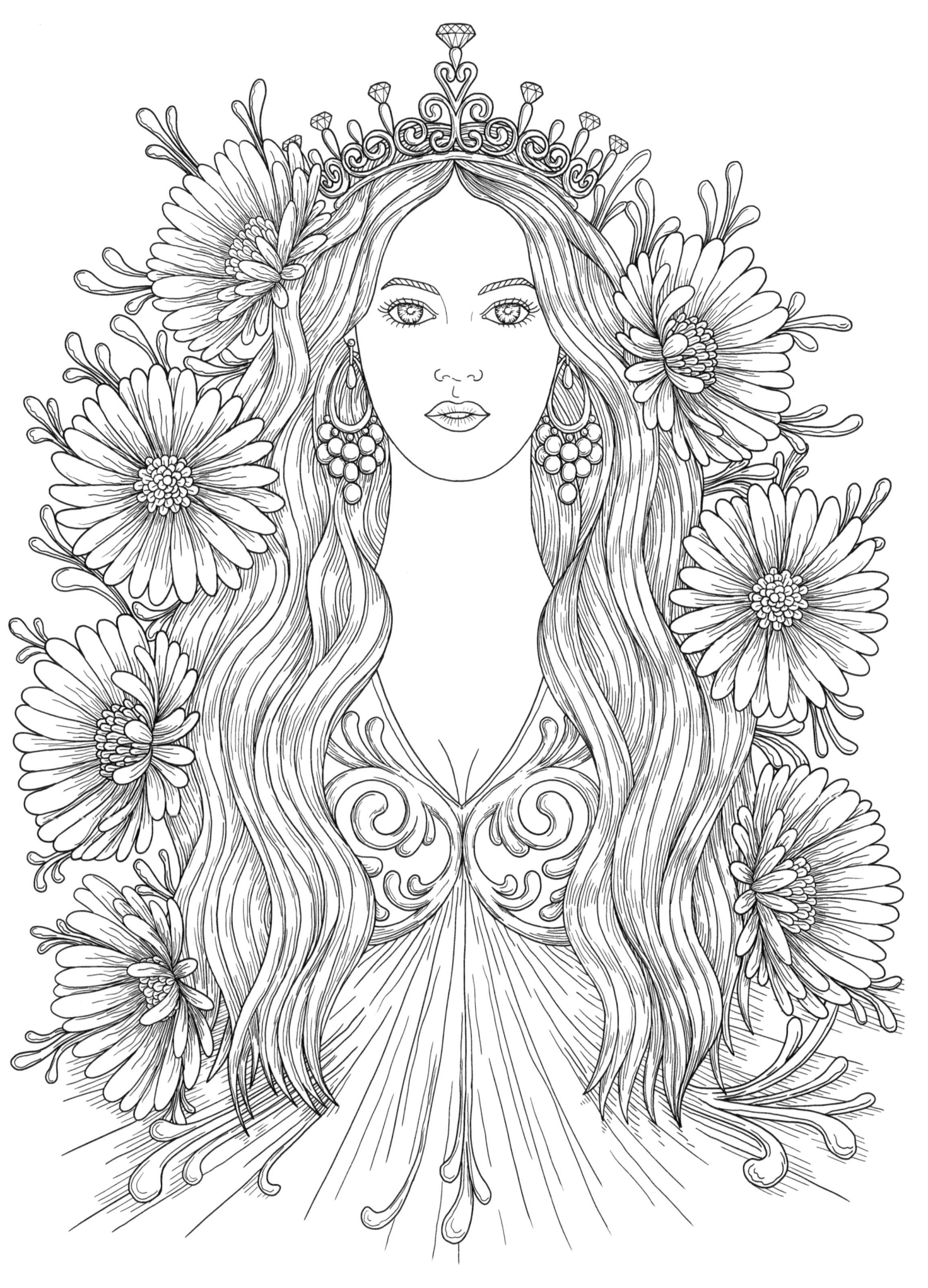

Byzantine Reign

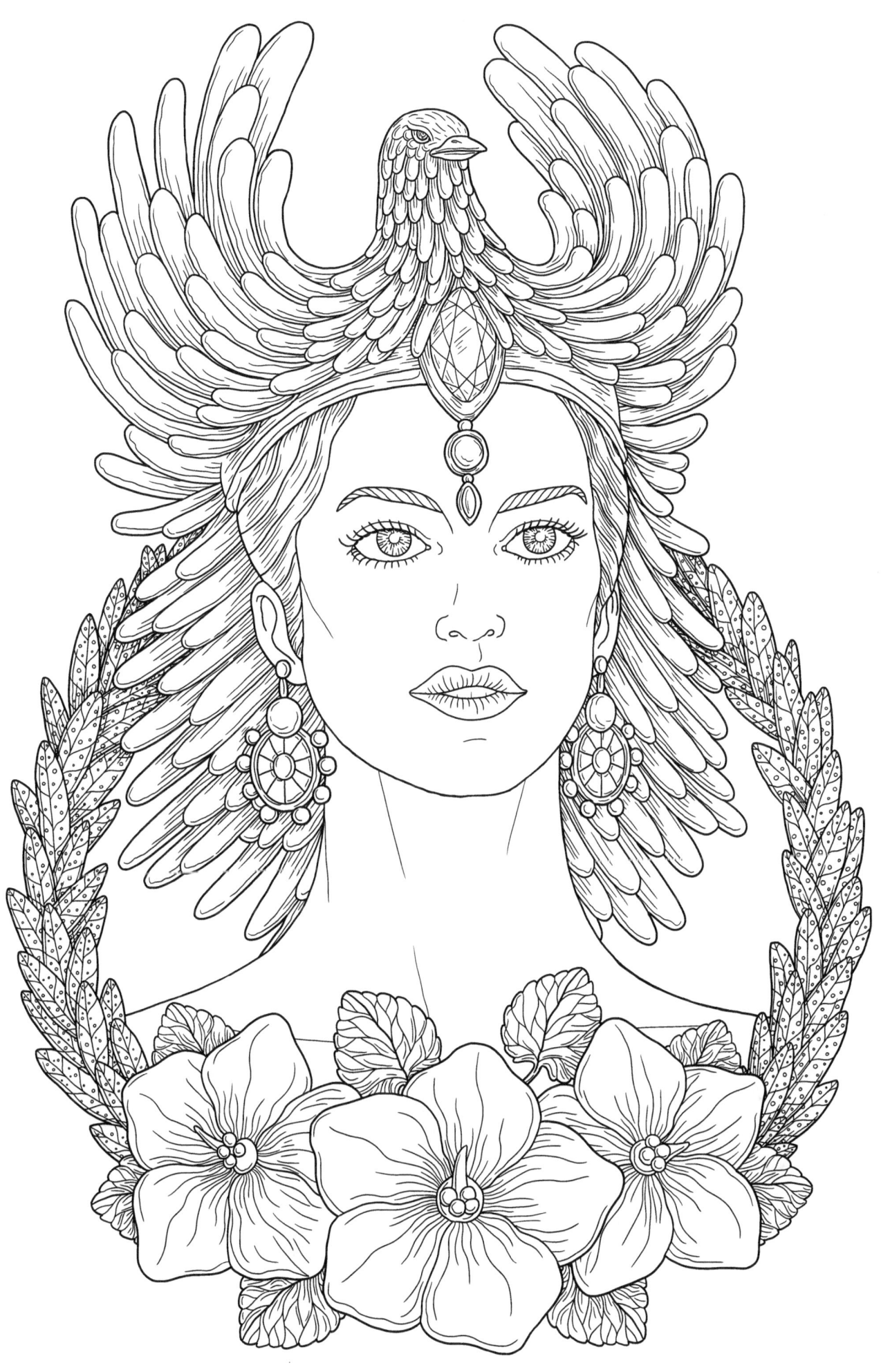

Mother-Daughter

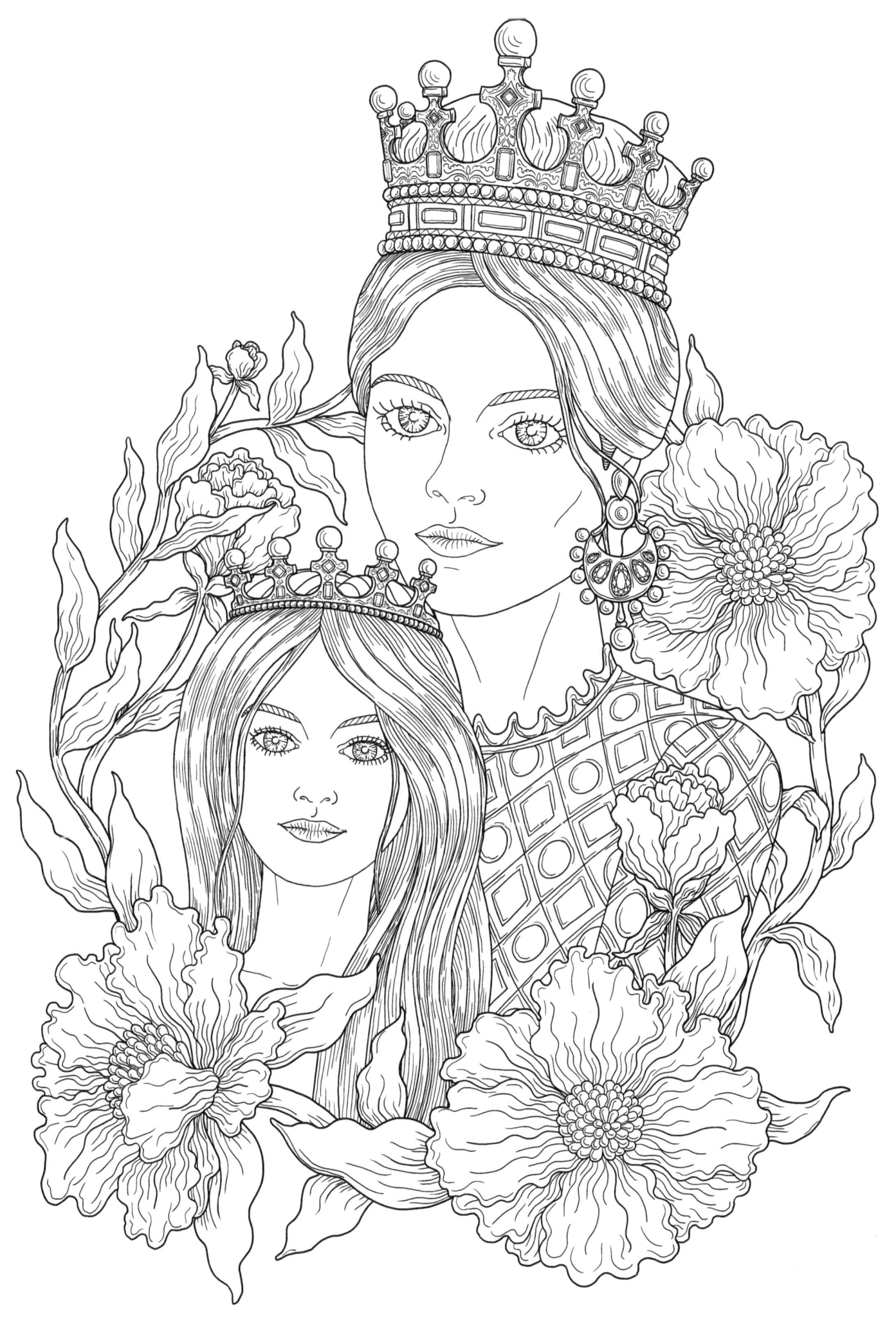

Butterfly Monarch

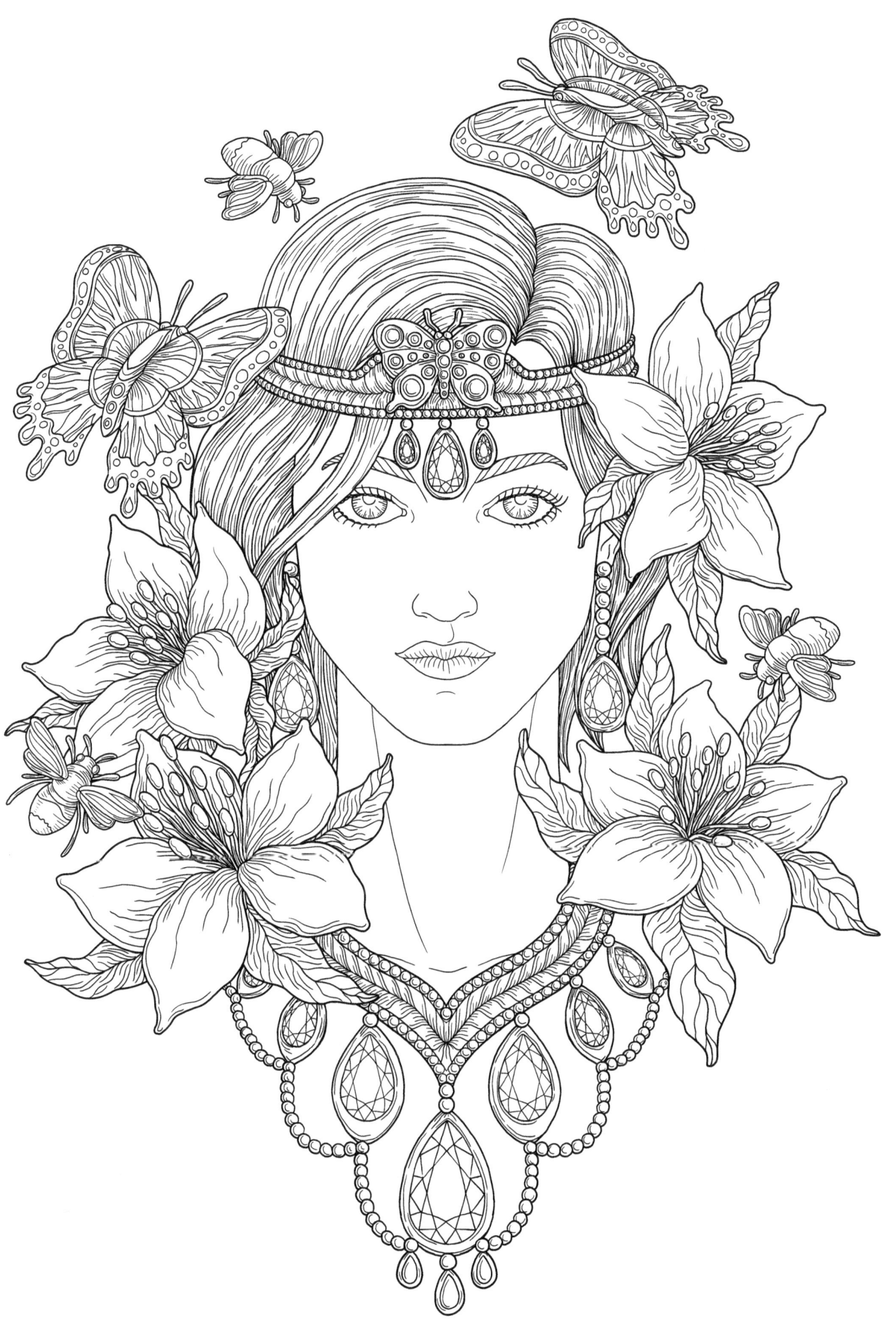

Metamorphosis

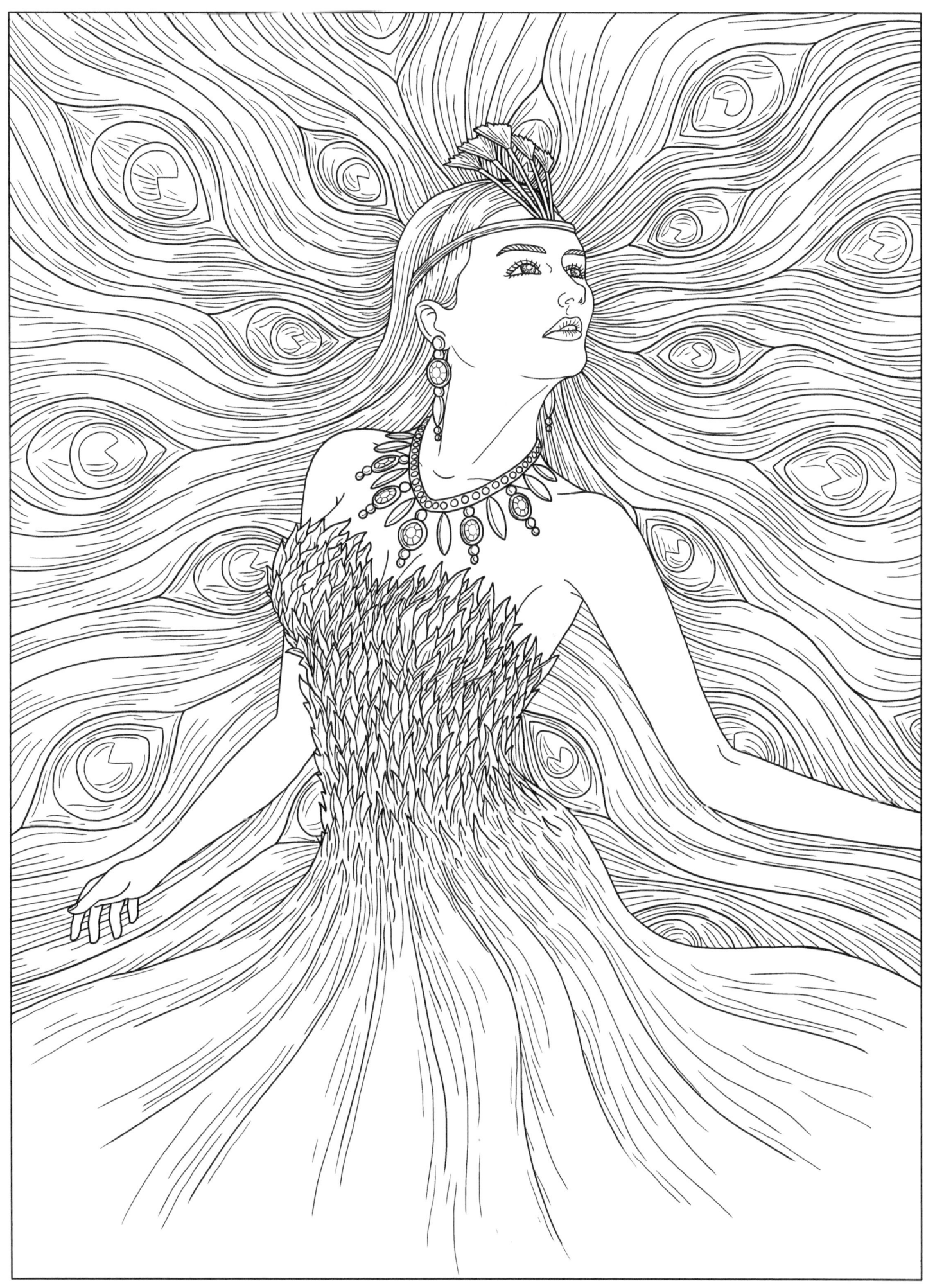

Native Night

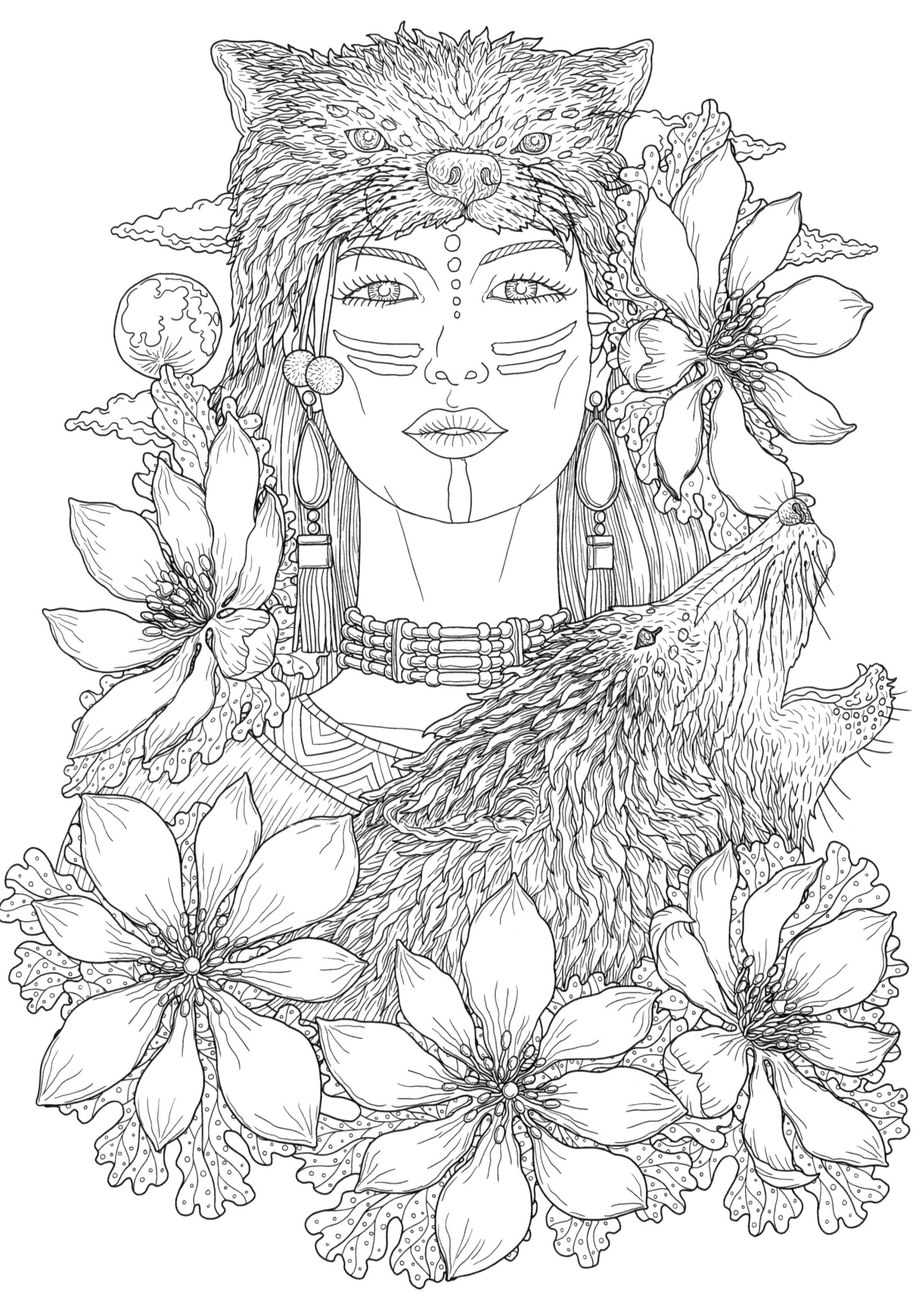

Great Horned King

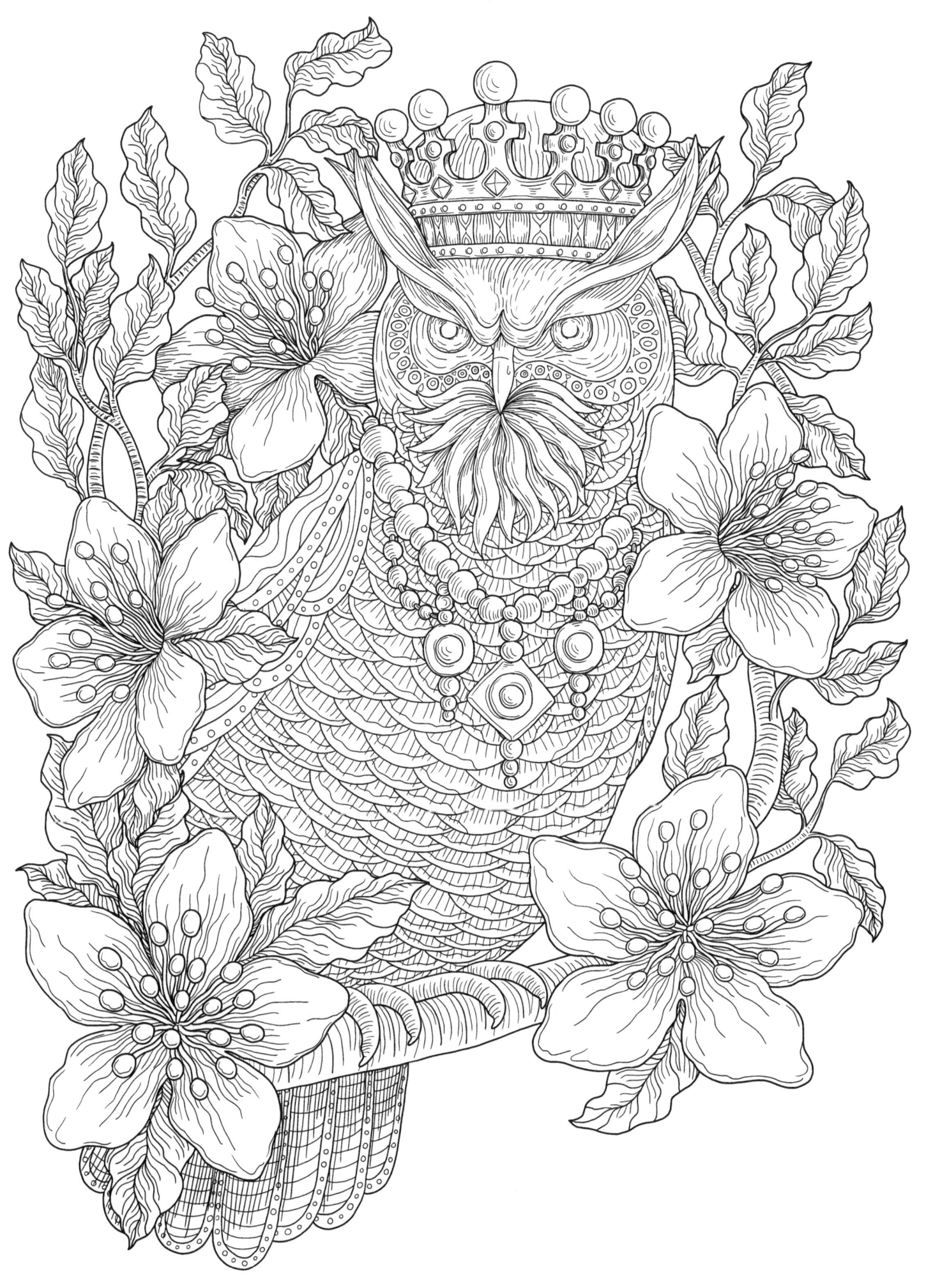

Empress Scarab

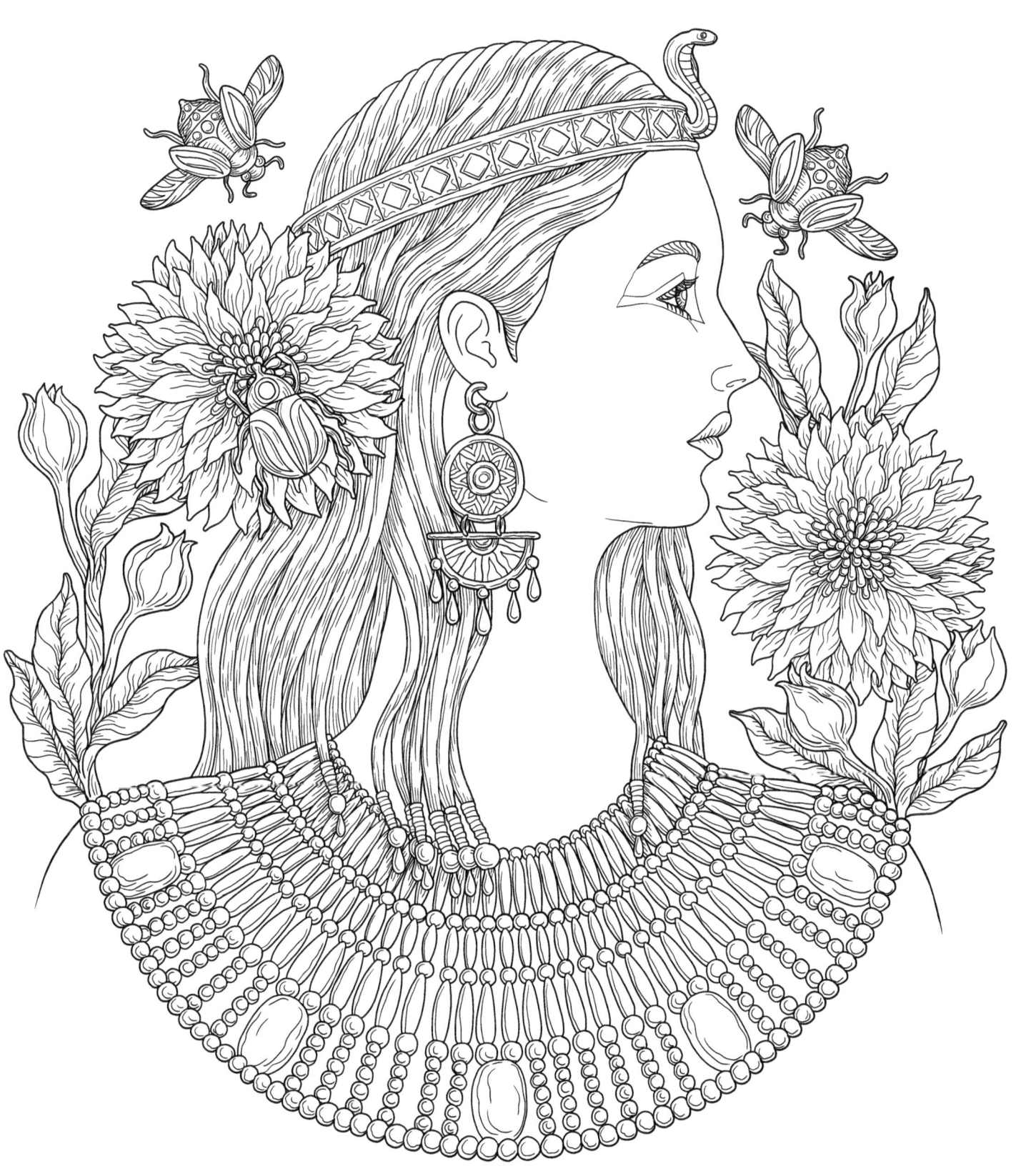

Lotus Rise

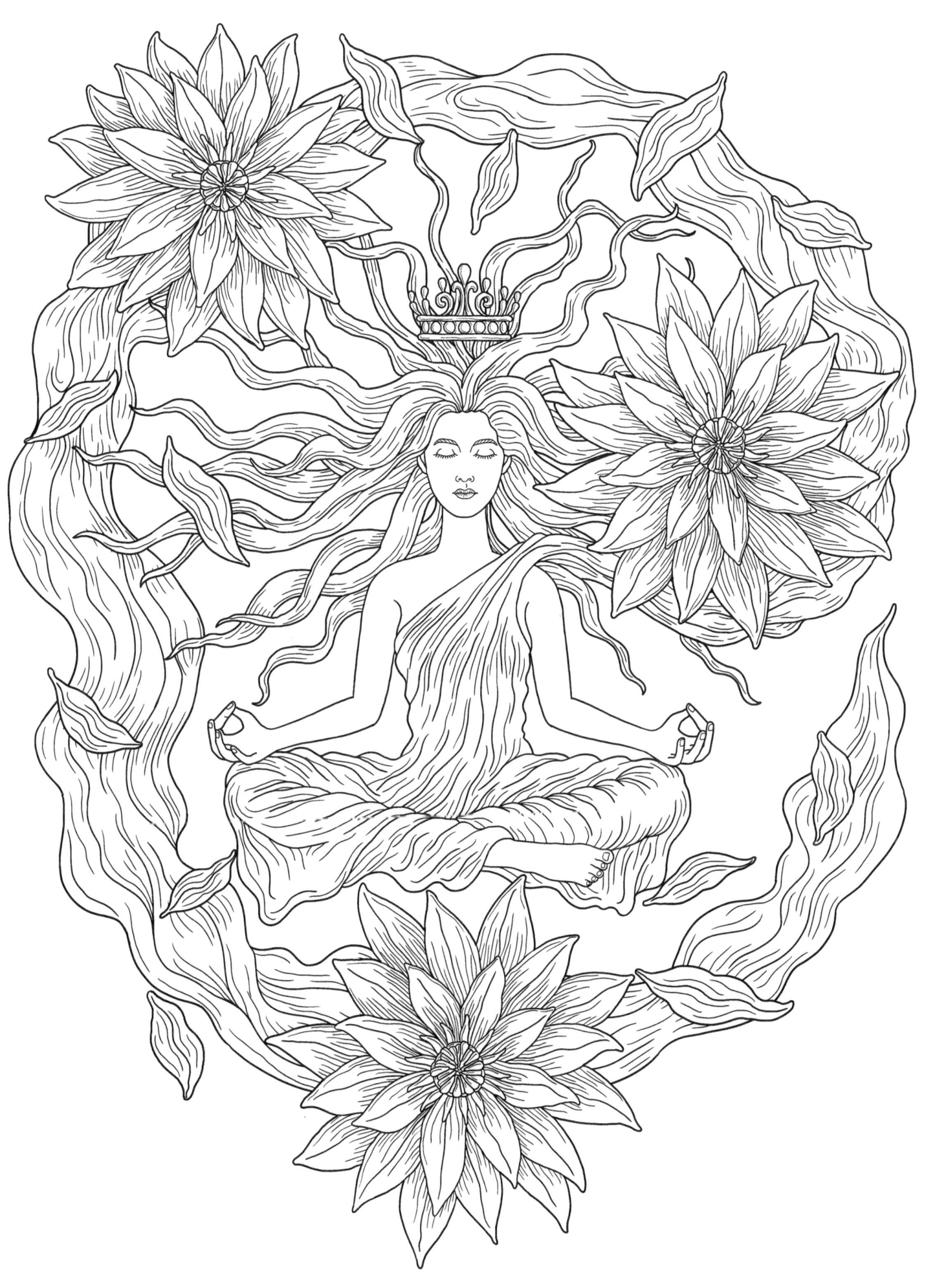

Rosemallow Blues

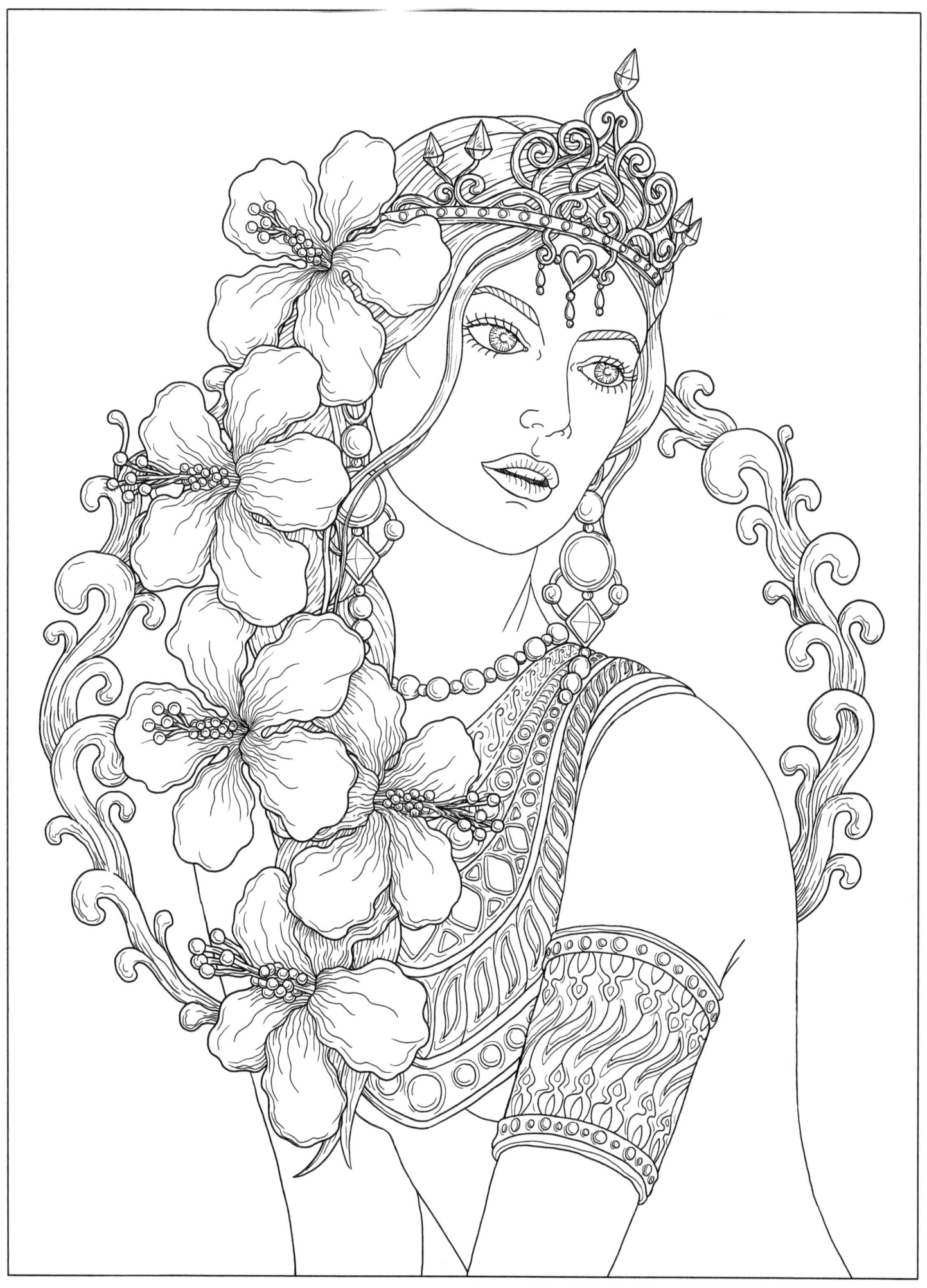

Garden Rose

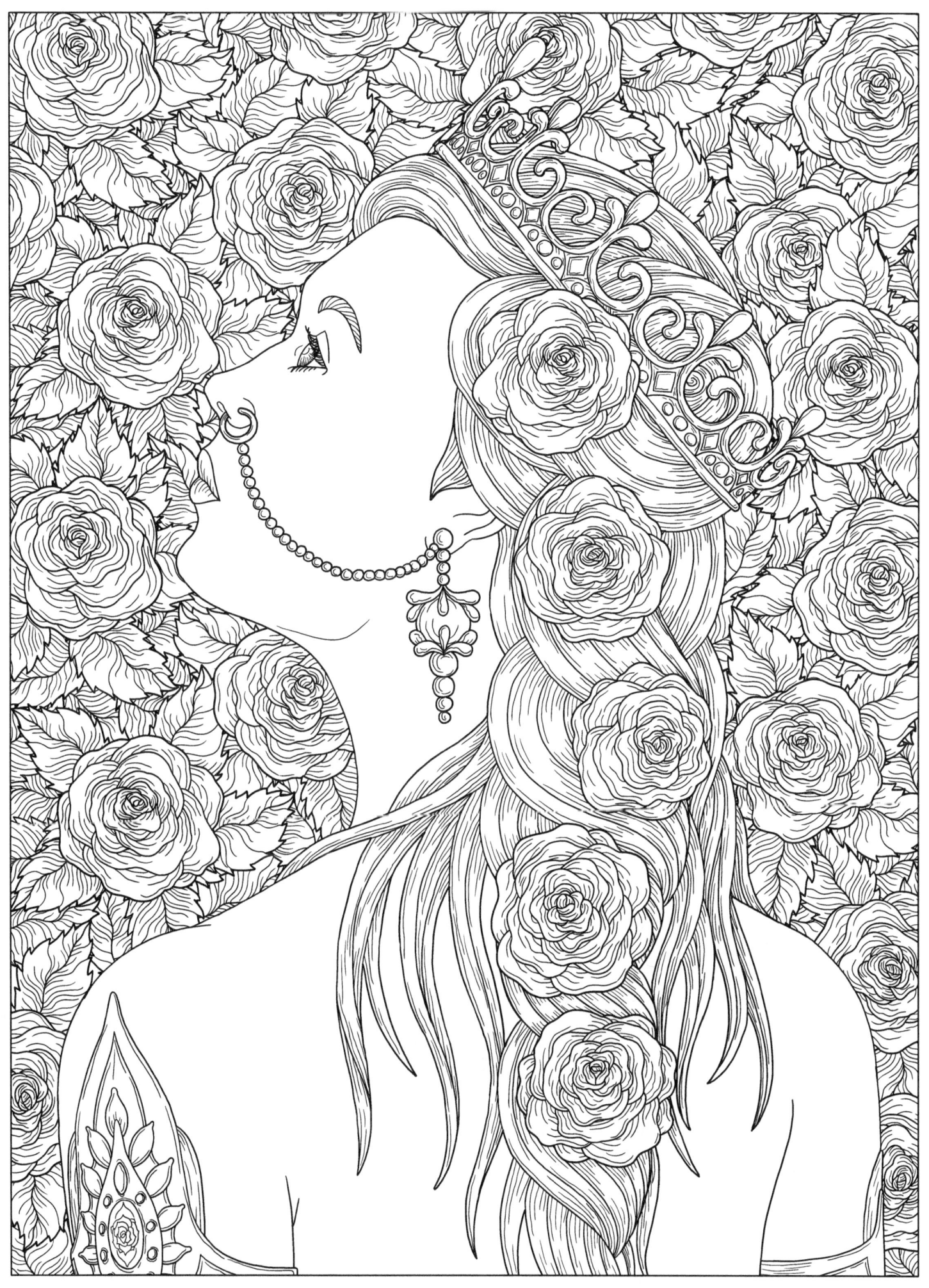

Bird Keeper

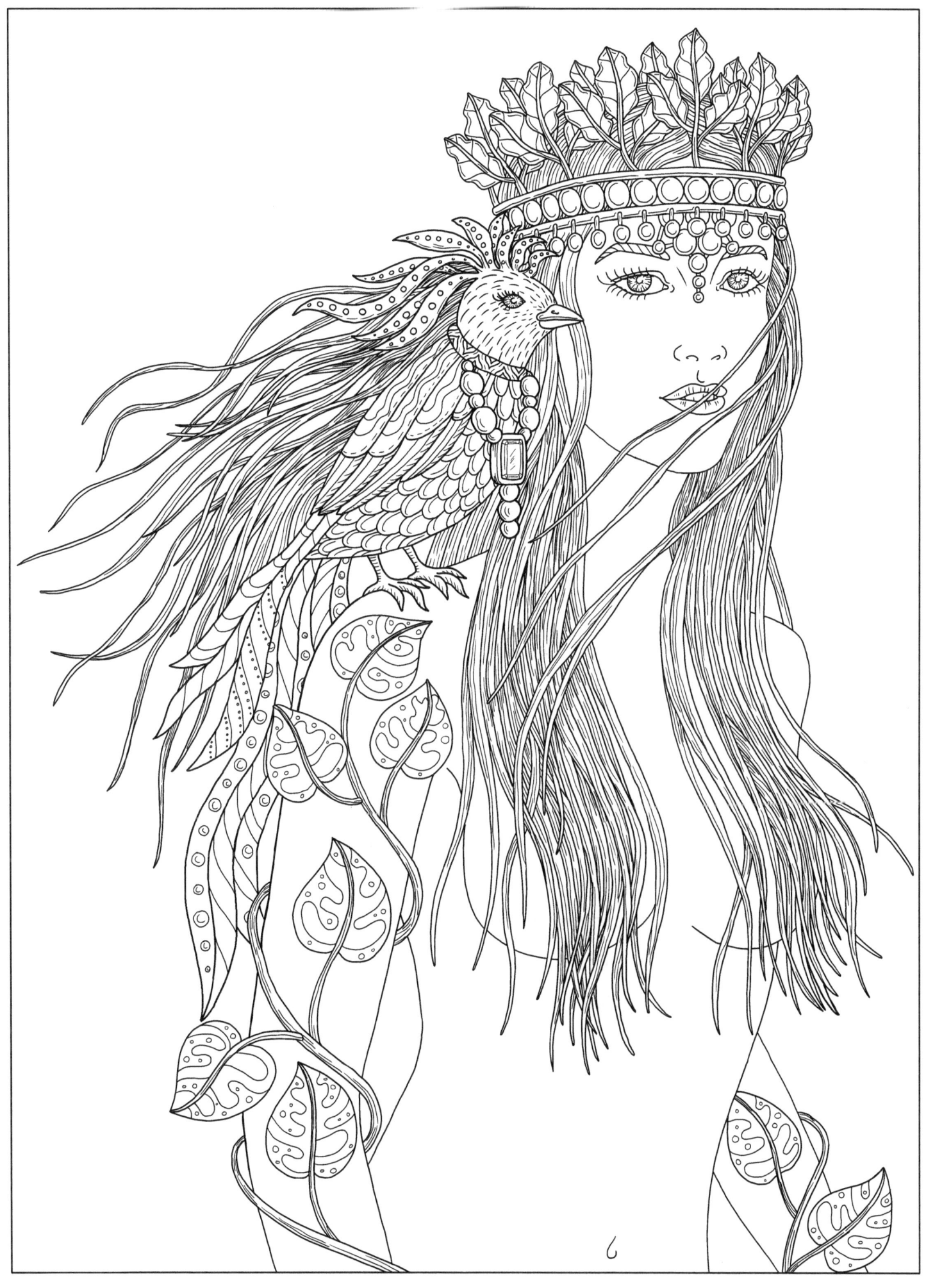

Feathered Friends

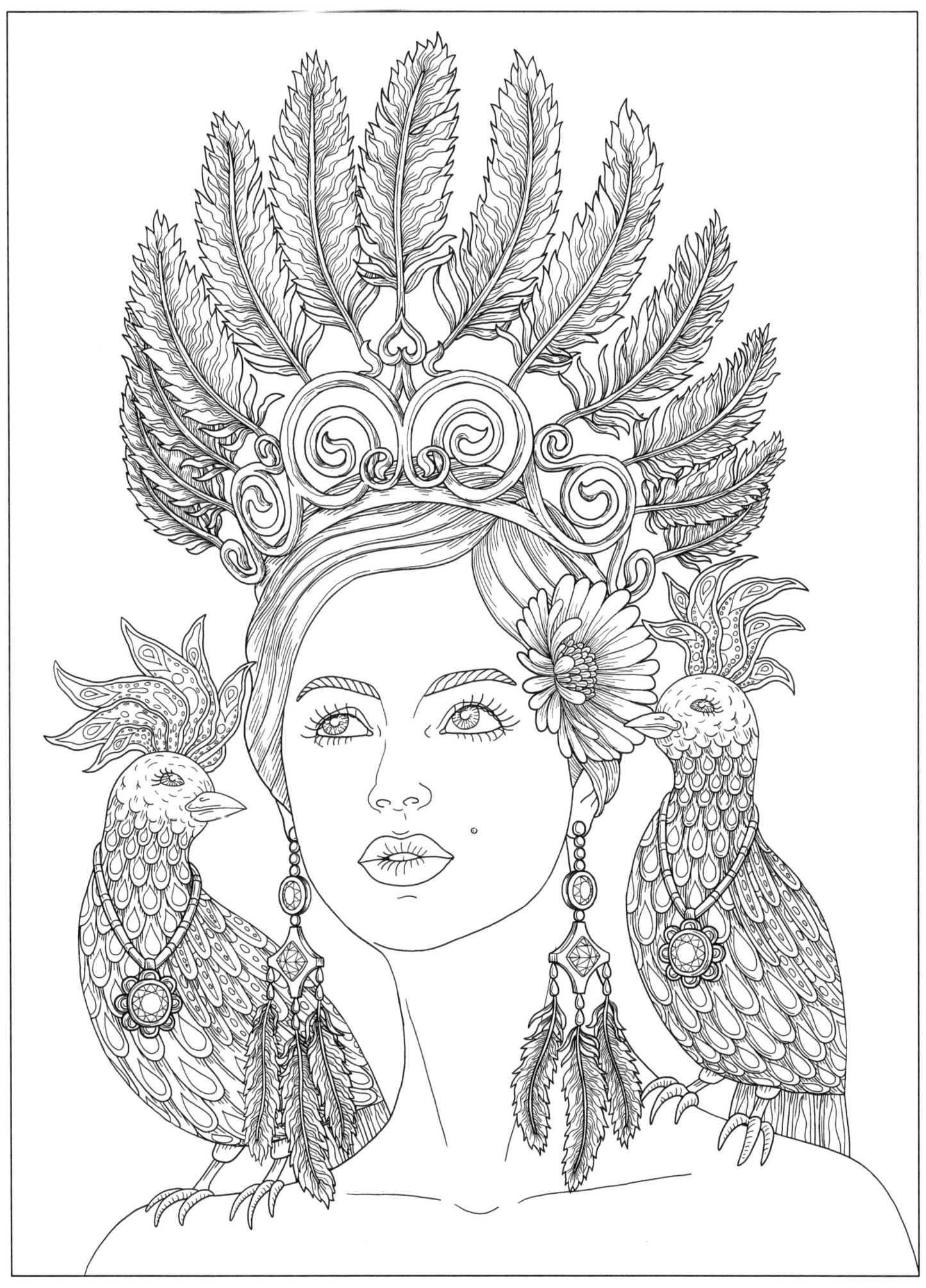

Royal Guard

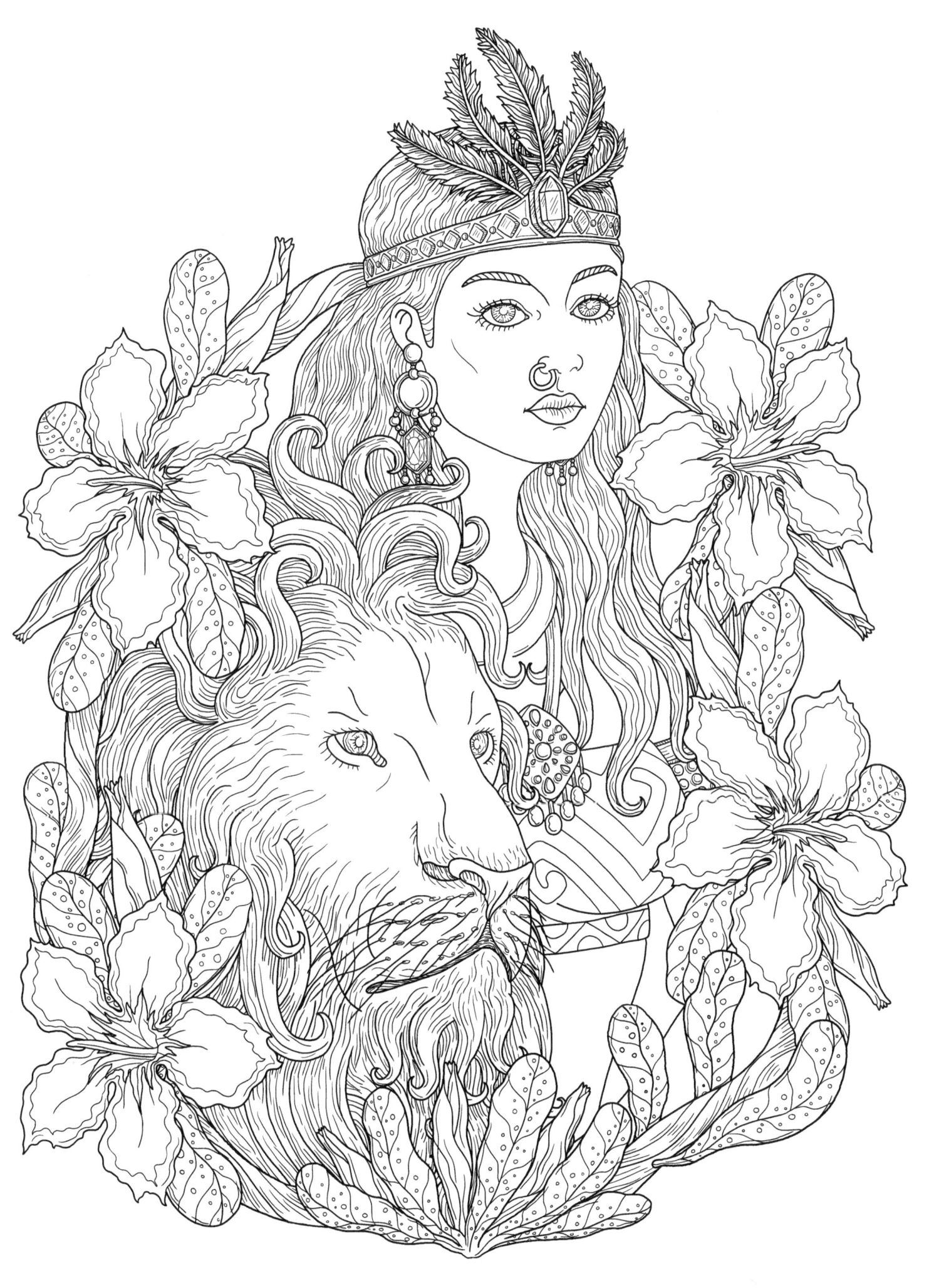

Glowing Night

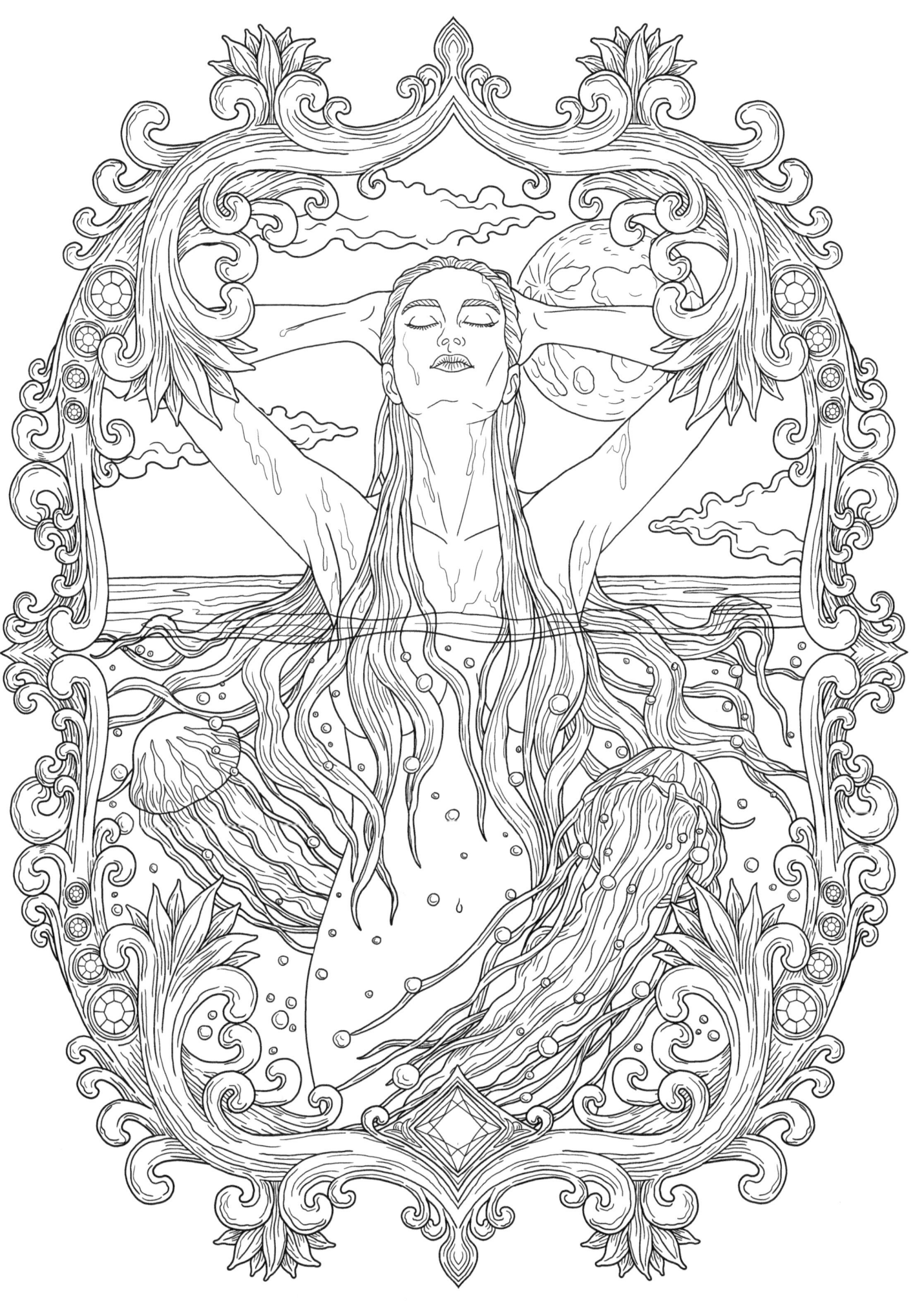

Trochili Paradise

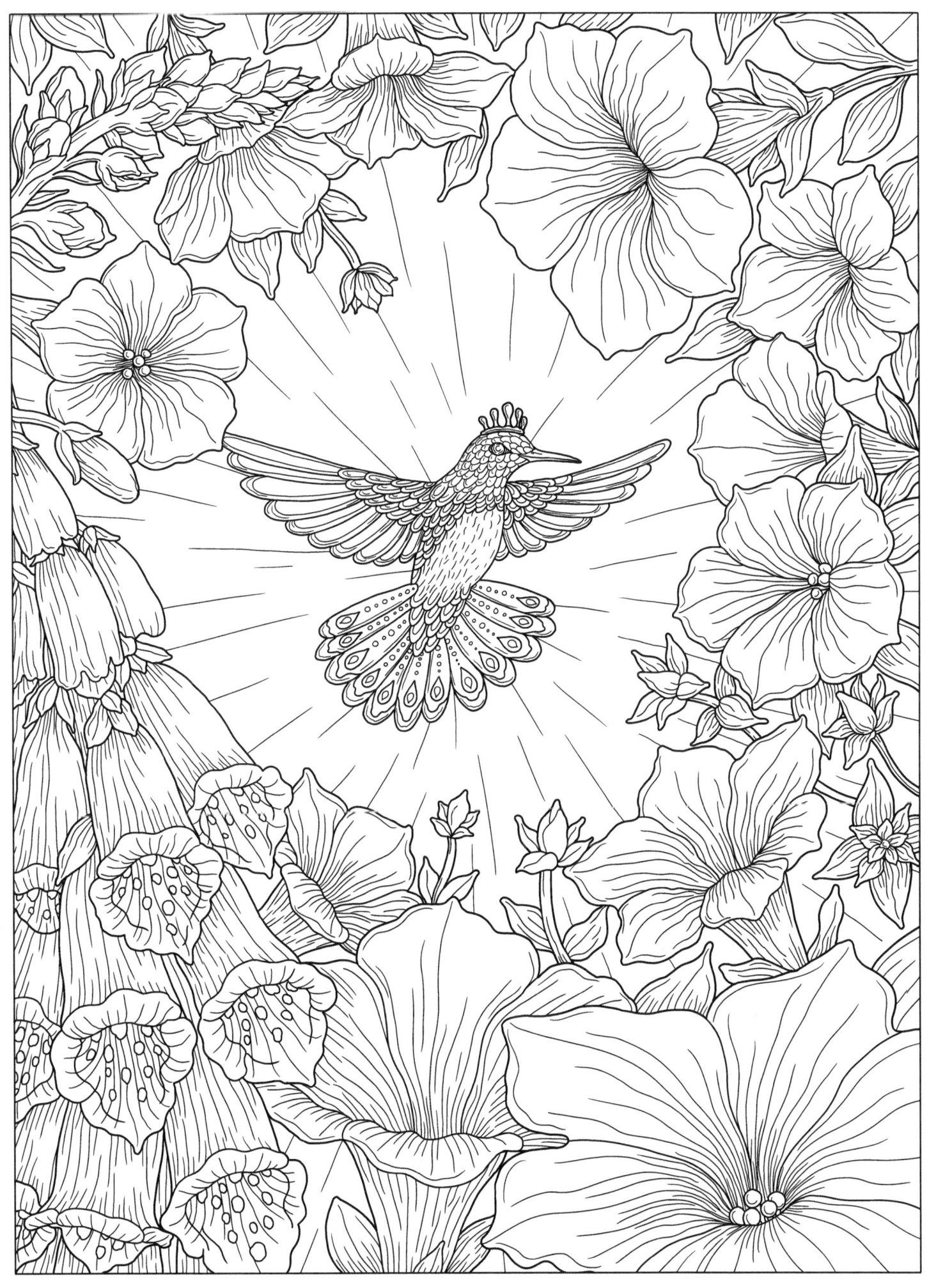

Lion Majestic

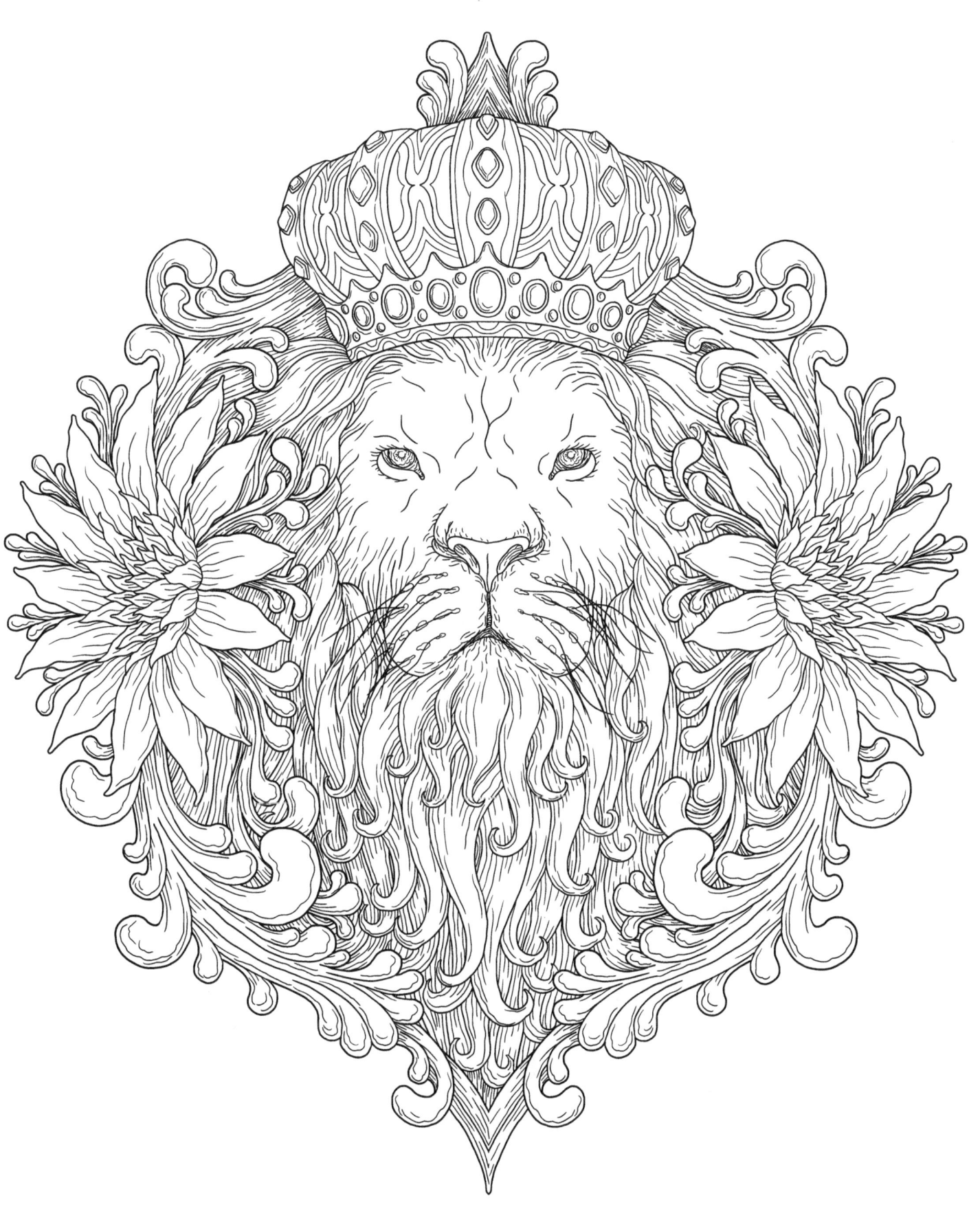

Viper Guardian

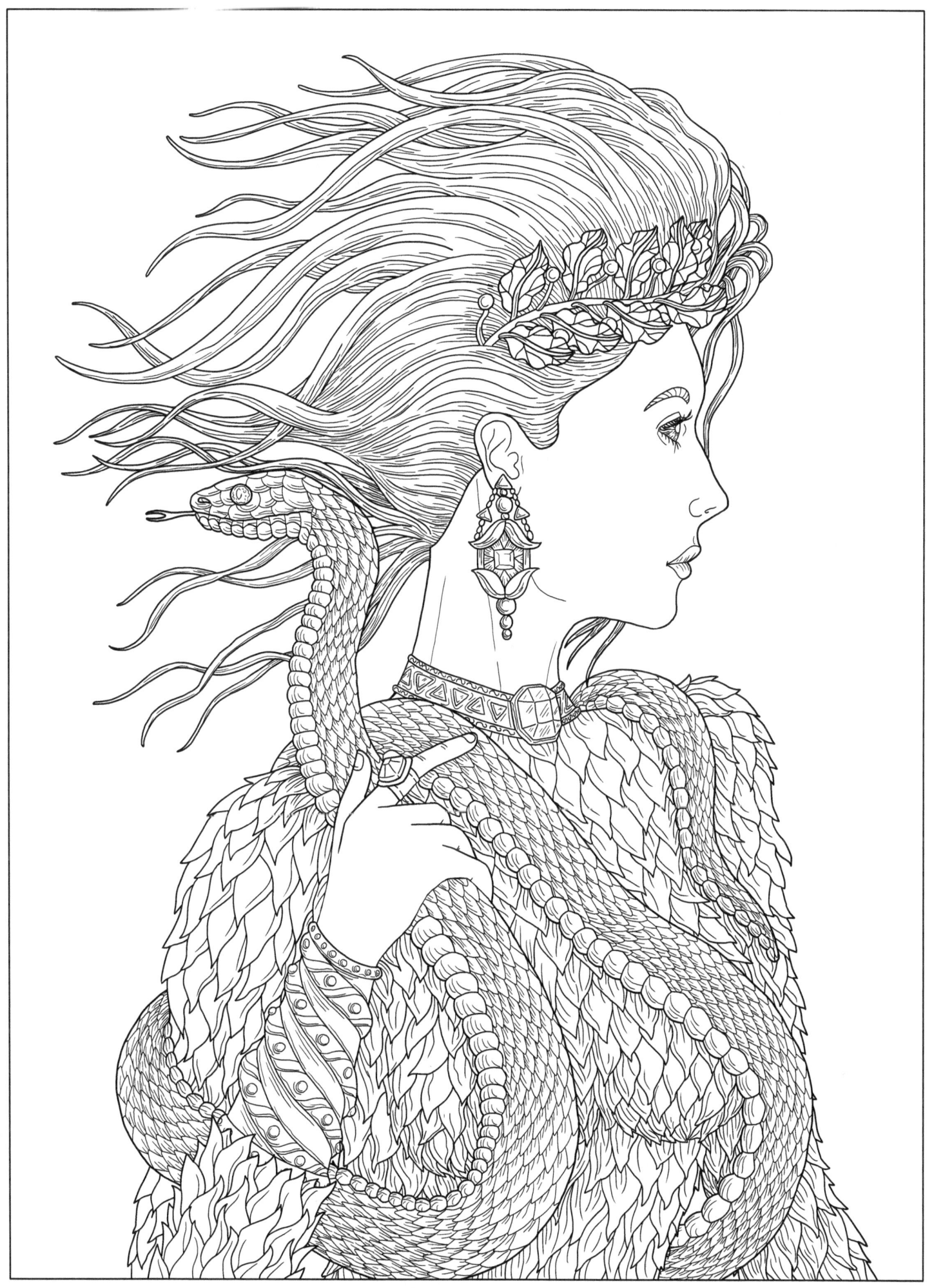

Water's Lily

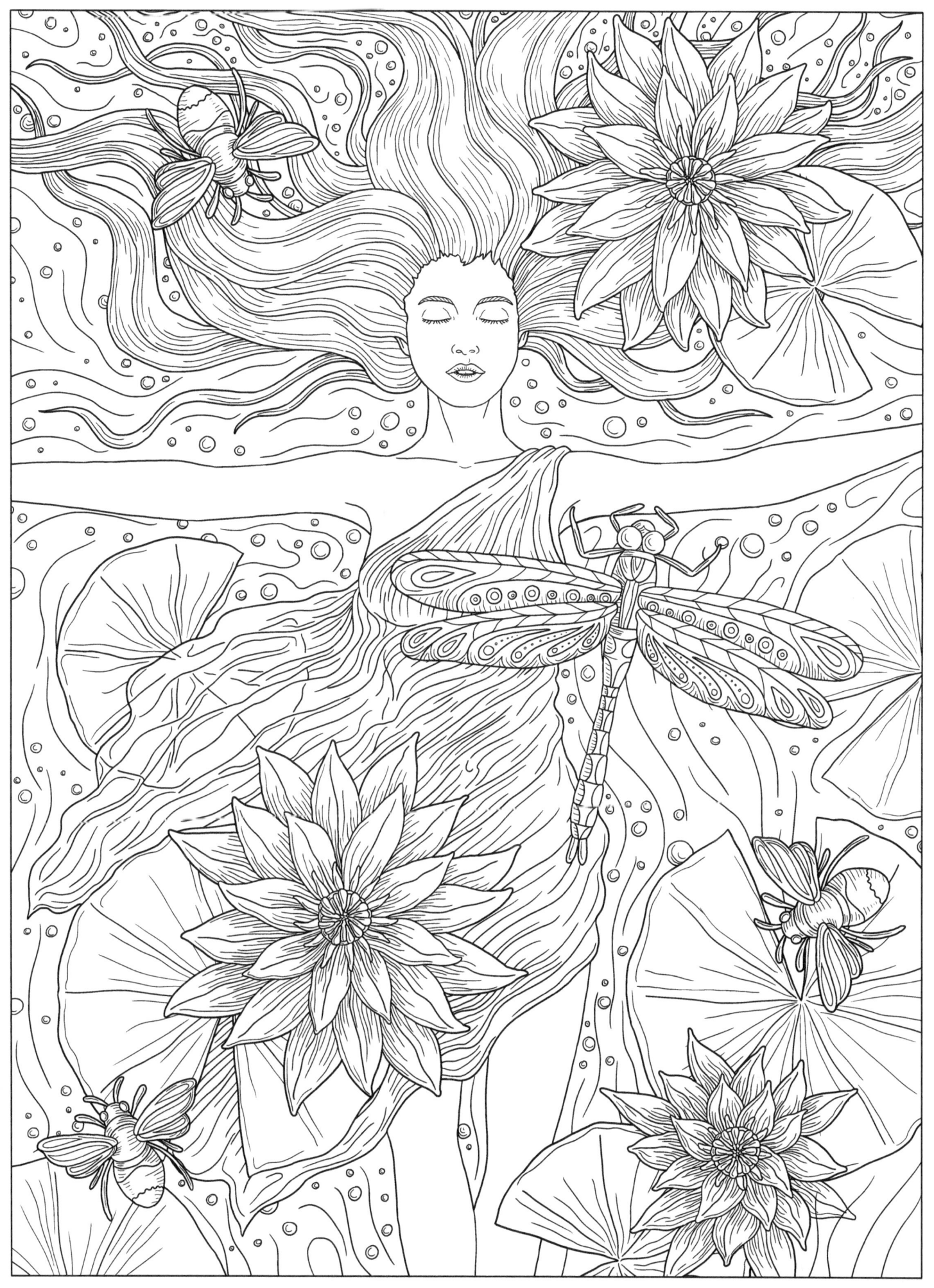

Lake Hypericum

Hepatica Dream

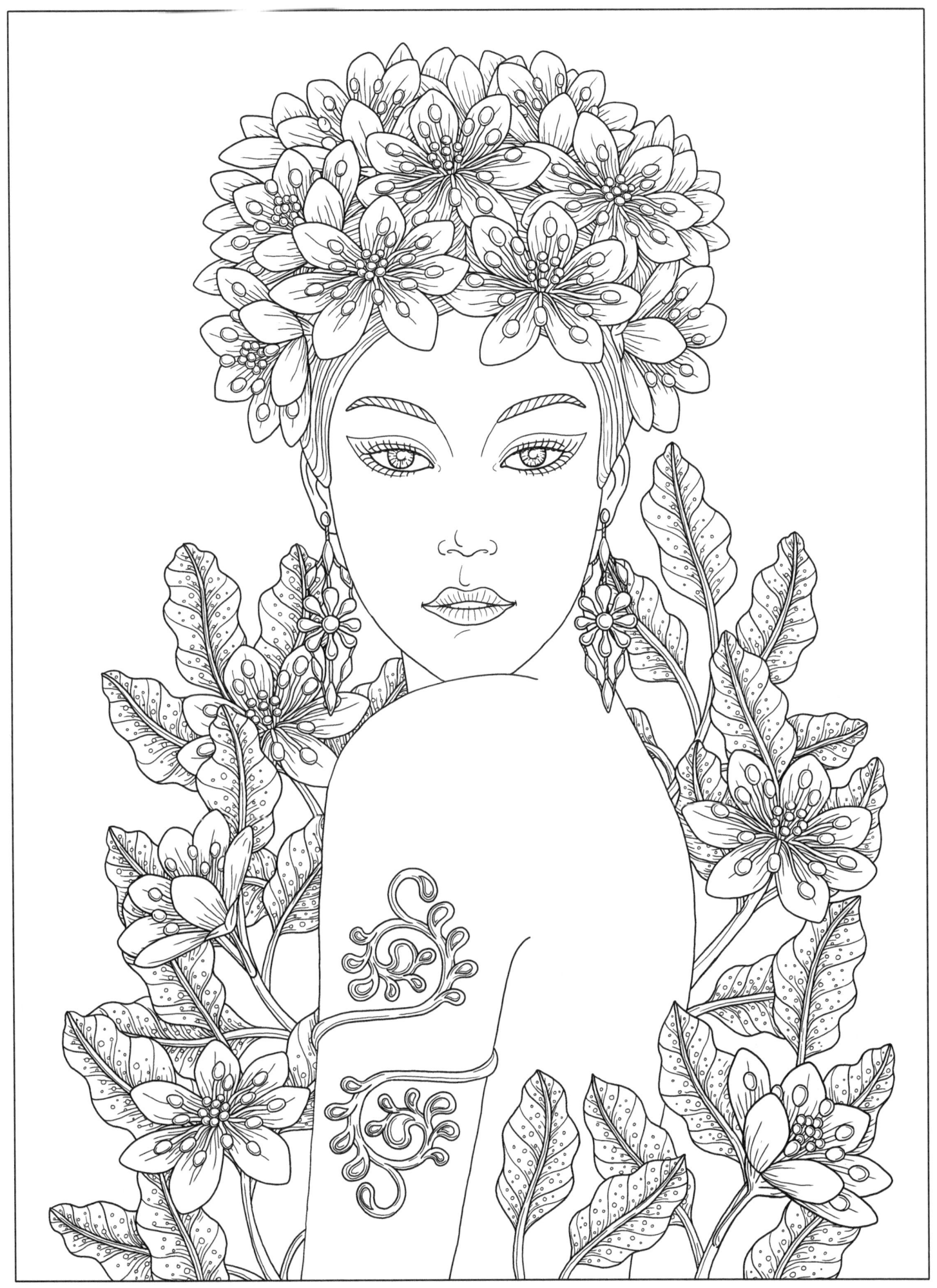

Tiger Lily

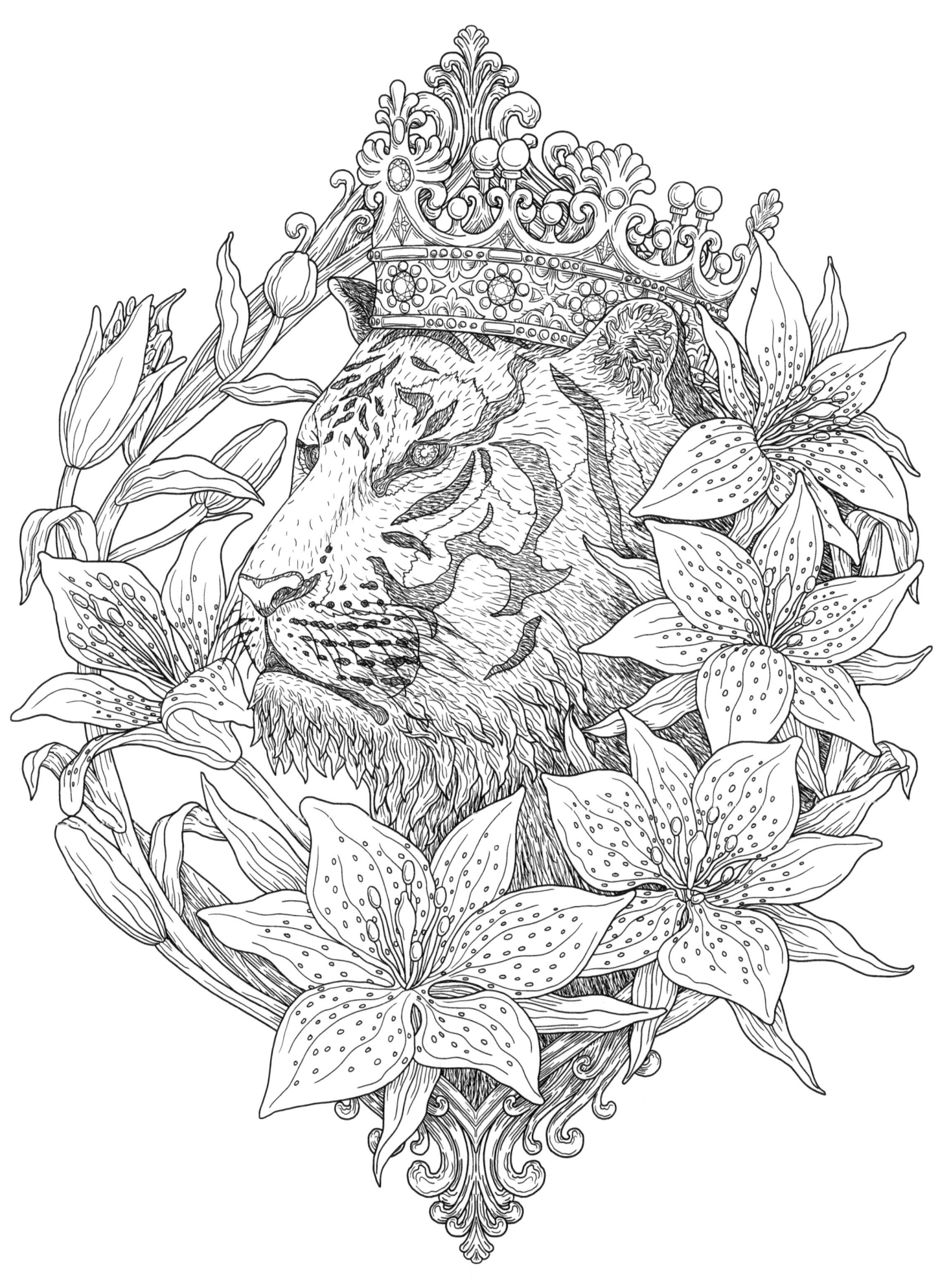

Raven Ruler

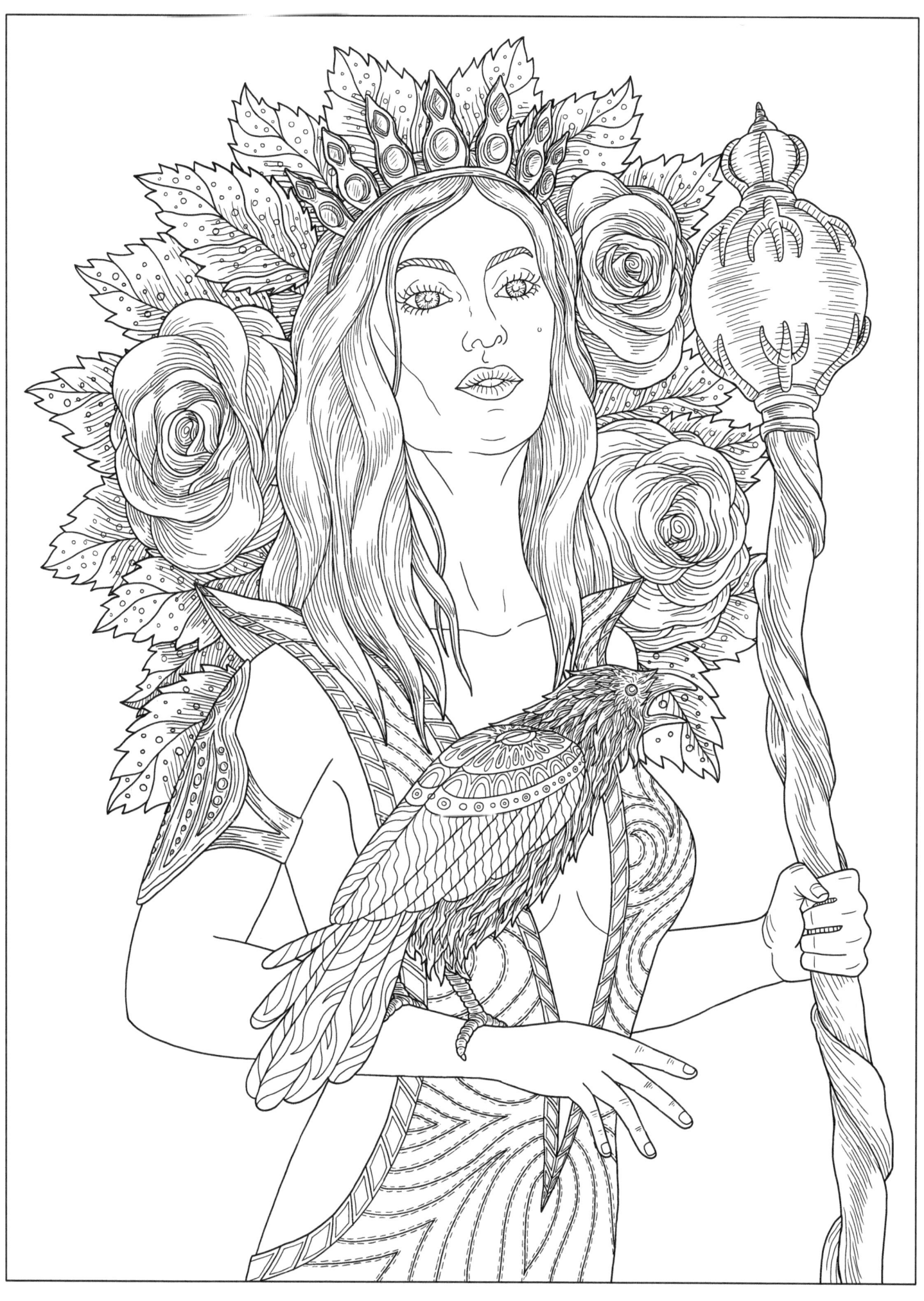

Volant Fantasy

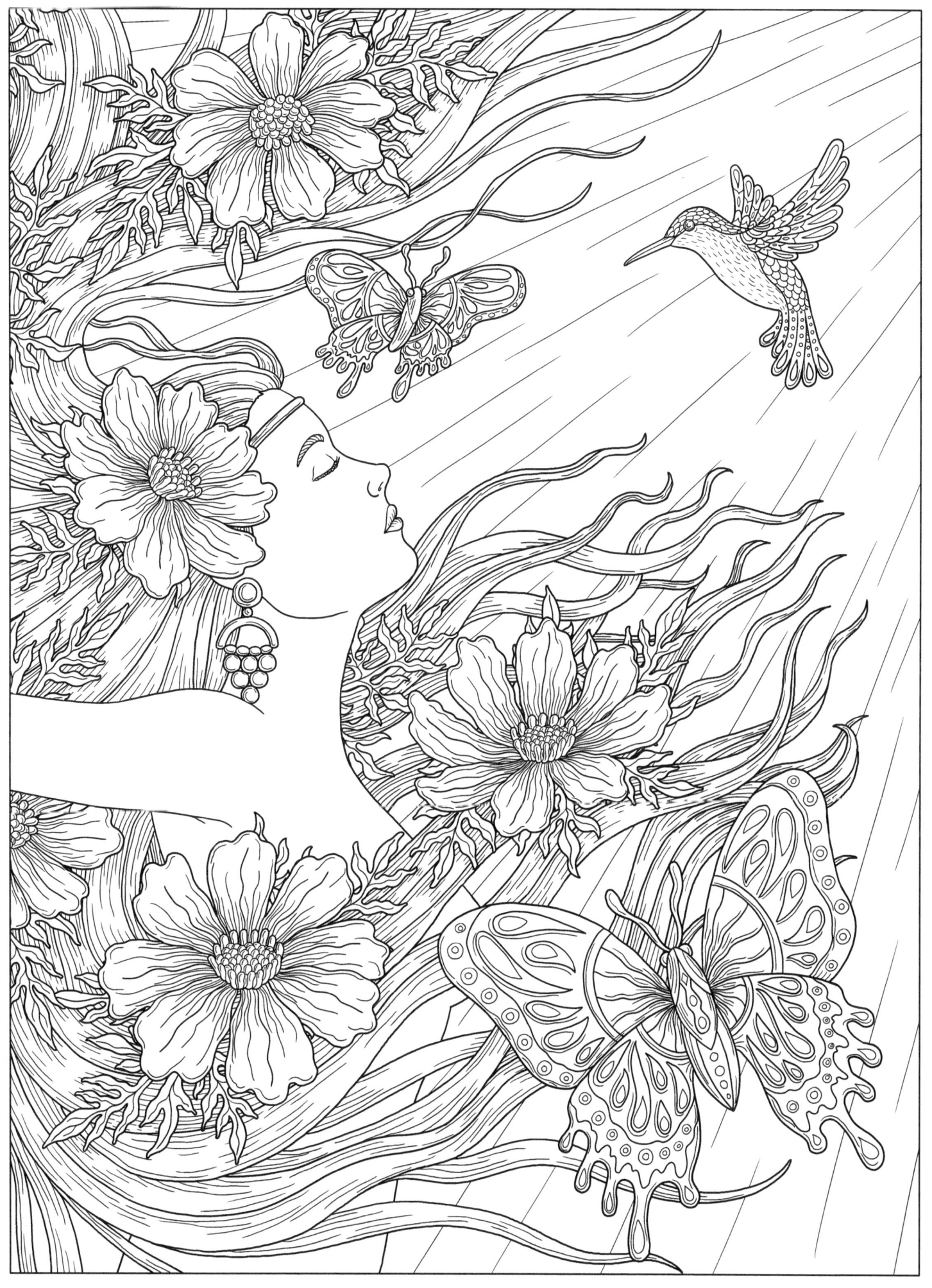

ALSO AVAILABLE FROM VIVID PUBLISHERS

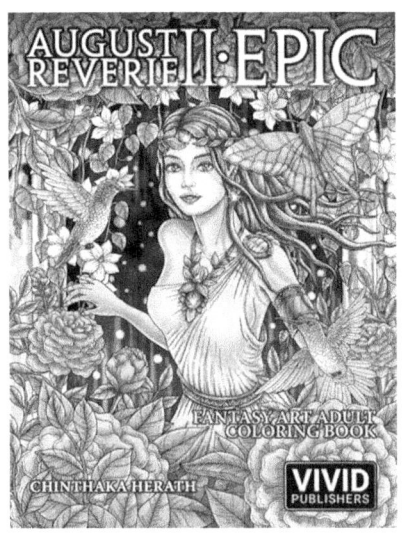

August Reverie 2: Epic

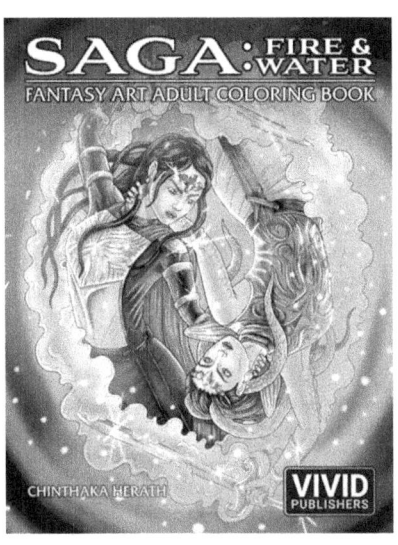

Saga: Fire & Water

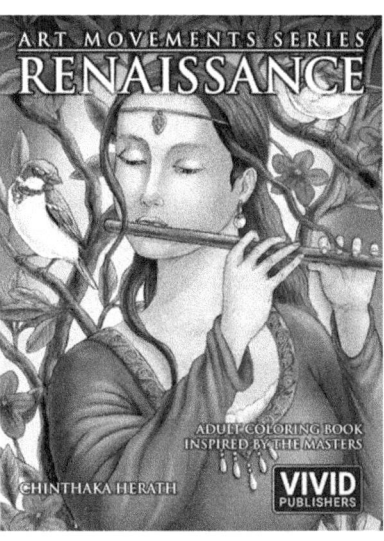

Art Movements Series: Renaissance

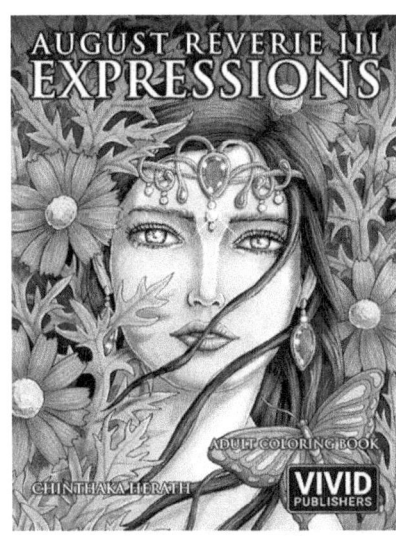

August Reverie 3: Expressions

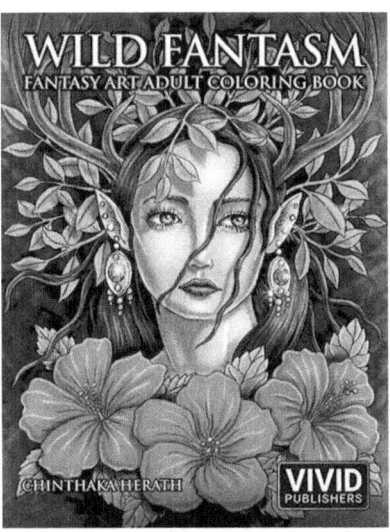

Wild Fantasm

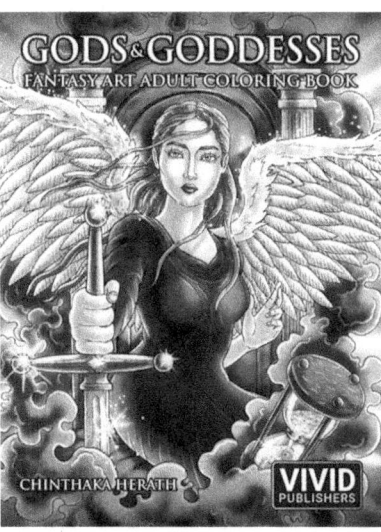

Gods & Goddesses

Preview all the pages at www.vividpublishers.com/books

www.ingramcontent.com/pod-product-compliance
Lightning Source LLC
Chambersburg PA
CBHW062159220526
45470CB00009B/2872